IN THEIR OWN WORDS

WORLD WAR II
LIFE ON THE HOME FRONT

A Primary Source History

Dear Son:—
How ar
you well I hope. It
very hot here now. W
miss you very much
know you do us. l
glad that you received
the money. How do y
like working in the
ware house. You say t
it keep you off of K.
duty. Will be glad w
you get sent to a base

Fiona Macdonald

Gareth Stevens
Publishing

CONTENTS

INTRODUCTION

INVASION ROUTES

→ GREATER GERMANY
→ SOVIET UNION

0   100
Miles

BALTIC SEA · LITHUANIA · LATVIA · KOVNO · VILNA · KOENIGSBERG · MINSK · DANZIG · EAST PRUSSIA · GRODNO · NAREW · BIALYSTOK · SOVIET UNION · BERLIN · GREATER GERMANY · POZNAN · WARTA · WARSAW · VISTULA · LODZ · BREST-LITOVSK · LUBLIN · KOVEL · POLAND · KRAKOW · LVOV · PROTECTORATE OF BOHEMIA AND MORAVIA · SLOVAKIA · HUNGARY · ROMANIA

GERMAN FORCES INVADED POLAND SEPTEMBER 1, 1939

SOVIET UNION OCCUPIED EASTERN POLAND SEPTEMBER 7, 1939

Above: *A map shows the routes of the German invasion of Poland, which led to Britain's declaration of war against Germany in 1939.*

Between 1939 and 1945, the world was at war. It was a terrible conflict, causing more deaths and suffering than ever before. More than 50 countries were caught up in the fighting; many others were indirectly involved.

World War II started in 1939. It was first fought only between the Allied nations of Britain and France against Germany. By 1940, Germany had been joined by Japan and Italy. Together, those three countries were known as the Axis powers. The Axis powers were supported by Spain, Portugal, Switzerland, Romania, Hungary, and other European nations. The Allied powers were aided by their overseas colonies.

Early in the war, Joseph Stalin (1879–1953), the leader of the Soviet Union, had signed a pact of nonaggression with Adolf Hitler (1889–1945), the chancellor of Nazi Germany. By the terms of that agreement, each country pledged not to invade the other. However, Germany broke that pact by invading the Soviet Union in 1942. After the invasion, the Soviet Union joined the Allied powers to fight against Germany.

At first, the United States was neutral in the war. By 1941, however, the United States joined the Allied powers. That decision to enter the war followed the bombing by Japan of the U.S. naval base at Pearl Harbor, Hawaii, on December, 7, 1941. At the same time, China was invaded by Japan after expressing support for the United States.

Left: *British Prime Minister Winston Churchill (1874–1965) encourages civilians with his famous "V for Victory" salute.*

CIVILIAN THREAT

World War II was the first time that large attacks deliberately targeted civilians. Tragically, civilians suffered more than half the deaths and injuries of the war. Targeting people in this way was against international law, but government officials ignored that fact in their struggle to win the war.

German air raids on London, a series of bombings known as the blitz, were designed to wear down Britain's will. Likewise, the bombings of Dresden, Germany, and Tokyo, Japan, killed hundreds of thousands of civilians as the Allies tried to end Axis resistance. The final blow to Japan came in August 1945. Shortly after Germany surrendered, the United States dropped atomic bombs on the Japanese cities of Hiroshima and Nagasaki. Hundreds of thousands of civilians

Above: German dictator Adolf Hitler (center) is welcomed by crowds at a Nazi rally in 1938.

Below: U.S. President Franklin D. Roosevelt (1882–1945, left), Vice President-elect Harry S. Truman (1884–1972, center), and Vice President Henry A. Wallace (1888–1965) were photographed in 1944. Fears over Roosevelt's poor health led him to replace Wallace with Truman. Roosevelt died in 1945, before the end of the war, leaving Truman to make the decision to drop the atomic bomb on Japan.

Above: A patriotic pin displays a wartime slogan and the flags of Britain and the United States, two of the Allied powers.

Above: *Polish Jews are lined up a Warsaw ghetto in 1942.*

Below: *This is the entrance to the concentration camp at Auschwitz-Birkenau. It is estimated that between 1.1 and 1.5 million people died there between 1940 and 1945.*

were killed. Many more died later of radiation sickness. The will of Japan was broken, and the Japanese government surrendered. Civilian deaths had mounted across German-occupied countries in Europe. Hitler's Nazi regime had murdered millions of people as part of their plan to rid Europe of "undesirables," people the Nazis deemed social outcasts, political enemies, or threats to their vision of a racially "pure" German state. The Nazis believed that Jews, Roma (Gypsies), Poles, Russians, and other Slavic peoples were racially inferior to "pure" Germans. The targeted people had been rounded up and persecuted or killed. The Nazis' most deliberate plans for persecution, imprisonment, and finally extermination, however, had been aimed at Europe's Jewish population. In Europe, about 6 million Jews and an equal number of other civilians perished. That systematic extermination of Europe's Jews became known as the Holocaust.

It is impossible to calculate the total number of lives that were lost. Historians estimate that at least 35 million people died on the home front during the war. As many as 100 million more were injured. The largest numbers of civilians died in the Soviet Union (7-8 million), China (7.5 million), and in the Indian subcontinent (4 million). In Britain, about 90,000 civilians were killed, in France around 350,000, and in Germany, at least 880,000.

New technologies for bombs and biological weapons led to higher death counts. By the 1940s, engineers had designed planes that could carry heavy loads of bombs over long distances. Between 1940 and 1945, more than 30,000 bombers were built in the United States alone. Each raid caused massive fatalities.

In Asia, three million men and women were forced into slavery by Japanese invaders. Most of the slaves died. Japan was also the only country to use biological weapons. The Japanese killed more that 200,000 Chinese civilians by bombing China with the germs of deadly diseases, such as botulism and anthrax. The Japanese also poisoned civilian water supplies with cholera and typhoid.

The war made normal life impossible. Millions of Europeans, Russians, and Asians ran short of food, or starved. The worst famine caused by the war was in Bengal (Bangladesh), where 1.5 million people died. Throughout Eastern Europe and the U.S.S.R., Soviet

Premier Joseph Stalin killed five million Russian citizens.

Soldiers and workers from the United States and Britain left home, sometimes for years, to fight thousands of miles away. The war strained families, as parents, children, husbands, and wives were divided.

Above: *An American soldier says good-bye to his wife and child in New York before heading to war.*

Right: *When American men went off to war, women became skilled employees who worked the jobs left vacant. "Rosie the Riveter" became a cultural symbol of female strength and patriotism during the war.*

7

Above: A racist Nazi poster accuses Jewish people of betraying Germany. It pictures a man lurking behind the flags of Britain, the United States, and the Soviet Union, and it reads, "Behind Enemy Powers: the Jew!"

Below: Well-trained German troops, pictured in 1936, became a symbol of Hitler's wish to rebuild Germany.

Six years before the start of World War II, in 1933, Adolf Hitler, Germany's new chancellor, broadcast a speech in front of his Nazi Party supporters. Crowds packed into the vast sports stadium in Berlin and shouted, "Heil!" and "Germany Awake!" Hitler outlined his plans for a new nation. Germany would be reborn! Its pride and economy would be restored through willpower, strength, and unity.

NEW HOPE

To millions of Germans, Hitler's speech offered hope and an escape from what he called "the dirt of the past 14 years." Life for German people had been difficult since Germany's defeat at the end of World War I (1914–1918). The victorious nations had forced Germany to disband its military, give up territory it had acquired during the war, and pay vast sums of money for the damage it had caused during the conflict. As a result, German industries collapsed. German currency became worthless. The German people felt humiliated and desperate.

ECONOMIC CRISIS

Germany's economic problems increased during the worldwide depression that began in 1929. Shops and factories closed. More than 5 million workers lost their jobs. German people were angry and resentful. They no longer trusted their government. The Germans searched for leaders with new ideas to make their nation great again. They chose Adolf Hitler.

SCAPEGOATS

Unhappy Germans blamed others for their hardships. Most of all, they blamed the Jews. For more than a century, Jewish families had played leading roles in German business, education, science, and the arts. Yet in Germany—and throughout much of Europe—Jews were often treated with disdain.

Hitler claimed that Jewish people "poisoned" Germany. He said that the nation could not grow strong again unless Jews were removed from Germany, along with other "outsiders," such as Slav and Roma people. Beginning in 1933, Jews living in Germany faced increasing discrimination. Jewish teachers,

> *"A state which in this age of racial poisoning dedicates itself to the care of its best racial elements must some day become lord of the earth."*
>
> **Adolf Hitler,**
> **Mein Kampf (My Struggle)**

doctors, and lawyers lost their jobs. Jewish businesses were closed down or vandalized. About half the Jews in Germany left their country; many went to the United States. Others sent their children abroad to better lives and never saw them again.

GREATER GERMANY

As well as rebuilding the German nation, Hitler wanted a Nazi empire, a "Greater Germany." He planned to create that empire by retaking land that Germans had occupied during World War I, and by conquering *Lebensraum* (living space) in Eastern Europe for "pure" (Aryan) Germans. In 1935, Hitler recruited half a million soldiers into a Nazi army, and ordered German factories to build planes, weapons, tanks, and warships. He established state contracts and built work camps. With those plans in place, Hitler sought to end unemployment and promote his Nazi ideas.

"Hitler came to power in 1933.... gradually, various problems arose. A difference was made between Aryan* and non-Aryan children. The Jewish children were told one day to sit at the back of the class.... The non-Jewish girls had to join the Hitler Youth ... they were taught all kinds of anti-Semitic [anti-Jewish] things and began to hate their old friends. I was hurt and puzzled. I had not changed, so why were they not my friends any more? Gradually, only the Jewish girls were my friends."

Susan Landsman, a Jewish girl in Nuremberg, Germany (*Aryan was a word used by the Nazis to describe white people of specific backgrounds.)

HITLER'S SUPPORTERS

In 1936, Hitler's Nazi troops took up positions in the Rhineland, a region of Germany that bordered France. That same year, German planes bombed peaceful civilians in the city of Guernica, Spain. In 1938, Nazi troops invaded Austria, the land where Hitler was born, and forced an *anschluss* (union) with Germany. At the same time, Hitler offered support to Francisco Franco,

Left: *Adolf Hitler appealed to the feelings of anger common in Germany after its losses of World War I.*

JANUARY 30, 1933
Adolf Hitler becomes the chancellor of Germany.

MAY 10, 1933
Nazi students burn books by Jewish writers.

JUNE 29–30, 1934
Hitler eliminates rival leaders during the "Night of the Long Knives."

SEPTEMBER 15, 1935
Nuremberg laws remove Jewish rights to citizenship and marriage.

SEPTEMBER 29, 1938
British Prime Minister Neville Chamberlain signs the Munich Agreement. Britain agrees it will not challenge Germany's claims to parts of Czechoslovakia.

OCTOBER 5, 1938
Passports belonging to German Jews are stamped with a J for "Jew."

NOVEMBER 9–10, 1938
More than 7,500 German Jews and Jewish businesses are attacked on *Kristallnacht* ("Night of Broken Glass").

DECEMBER 1938
Jewish parents in Germany, Austria, and Czechoslovakia send their children to safety in Britain and the United States.

Above: *Oswald Mosley (1896–1980), leader and founder of the British Union of Fascists, addresses supporters in London in 1934.*

Below: *London's Daily Express newspaper headlines read, "Peace!" after leaders of Germany, Britain, France, and Italy signed the Munich Agreement on September 30, 1938. The agreement allowed Germany to annex the Sudetenland, a region in the former state of Czechoslovakia.*

the dictator of Spain, and Benito Mussolini, the dictator of Italy. They shared Hitler's fascist goal to build mighty, unified, and intolerant nations. Mussolini became a military and political ally of Hitler throughout World War II until he was replaced by members of his own National Fascist Party in 1943. (Mussolini was executed by Italian resistance fighters in 1945.)

Franco's Spain managed to remain neutral during World War II, even though Franco received support from both Hitler and Mussolini. In fact, Franco was assisted by both leaders in his overthrow of the Spanish government during the Spanish Civil War (1936-1939). That conflict was incredibly violent. It made Franco the dictator of Spain. Meanwhile, in Japan, the warlike, nationalistic government began to conquer lands to build a Japanese empire.

APPEASEMENT

Hitler's rise to power and the strength of Germany's armed forces deeply worried many European governments, especially Britain and France. For most of the 1930s, they were anxious not to quarrel with Hitler. At the same time, Britain and France quietly prepared for war. Britain felt it could best protect its own safety by supporting Hitler.

Above: *Spanish artist Pablo Picasso (1881–1973) created a violent, anguished painting to express his horror at the bombing of Guernica, Spain, during the Spanish Civil War.*

TIME LINE
1939

MAY 22, 1939
A war alliance ("Pact of Steel") begins between Nazi Germany and Fascist Italy.

AUGUST 19, 1939
Germany sends U-boats to block the seas around Britain.

AUGUST 23, 1939
Hitler makes a pact of nonaggression with the Communist Soviet Union.

AUGUST 24, 1939
Britain calls up army reservists; British government takes on emergency powers.

In September 1938, Hitler and British Prime Minister Neville Chamberlain (1869–1940) met in Munich, Germany. Hitler promised peace in return for the Sudetenland, a region in Czechoslovakia where many German-speaking people lived. This pact was known as the Munich Agreement. Essentially, the agreement was blackmail, but Britain agreed not to dispute Hitler's claims.

Just six months later, however, Hitler broke his promise of peace with Britain. In March 1939, he sent his army to occupy the rest of Czechoslovakia. Shortly after, Hitler's ally, Italy's Mussolini, invaded Albania.

WAR IS DECLARED

On September 1, 1939, German troops attacked Poland, one of Britain's close allies. Two days later, supported by France, Prime Minister Chamberlain issued an ultimatum: "unless ... [the Nazis] were prepared at once to withdraw their troops from Poland, a state of war would exist between us." Hitler's army did not retreat. Britain and France declared war against Germany on September 3, 1939.

Left: *Two Axis leaders shake hands. Hitler (right) greets Italian dictator Mussolini.*

> "Historians will show that the German nation found its way back again to the position of an honorable great nation—that our history has once more become a worthy history."
>
> *Adolf Hitler, speech after signing the Munich Agreement, 1938*

Below: *In New York, a man holds a newspaper announcing the British declaration of war on Germany on September 3, 1939.*

Above: *This British shelter could sleep seven people. With Hitler's Nazi army advancing throughout Europe, British government officials provided emergency shelters for many families during World War II.*

GETTING READY

That same day, the war with Germany was announced to British civilians in a radio broadcast. People around the world felt frightened. They remembered the dreadful loss of life during World War I. Others supported Britain's decision to go to war with Germany. For the past two years, Britain had been preparing its citizens to face a possible conflict. Precautions against bombing raids included digging deep trenches in parks and playing fields. The British government also issued two million iron shelters for its citizens. Those were offered to poor people living in areas expected to be bombed by German aircraft. By 1939, British government officials also distributed 44 million gas masks to civilians to protect them against the possibility of attacks by poison gas.

KEEPING CONTROL

The British government also issued tough security measures to protect the country from potential spies. The first laws enforced the use of individual identity cards. A new Ministry of Information controlled the flow of news and issued government warnings or advice. Television broadcasts were stopped.

SEPTEMBER 1, 1939
Germany invades Poland.

SEPTEMBER 3, 1939
German submarines sink British passenger ship *Athenia*; Britain and France declare war on Germany.

SEPTEMBER 24, 1939
Food rationing begins throughout Europe.

Above: *Members of the all-volunteer British Home Guard practice fighting with bayonets in 1941.*

Newspapers were censored. Soon after the war began, in 1940, around 25,000 "enemy aliens"—innocent civilians living in Britain, but born in enemy countries—were rounded up and put in prison camps. Within time, most of those people were freed. As many as 7,000 people were deported from Britain, however.

FIGHTING FORCES

In Britain, a mandatory draft into the armed forces went into effect on September 2, 1939. All healthy men aged 18 to 41 were called upon to fight. Older civilians joined volunteer forces such as the British Home Guard, which had nearly a million members in 1940.

Below: *A card issued in packs of British cigarettes during the war explained how to correctly wear a gas mask.*

"We shall defend our island whatever the cost may be. We shall fight on the beaches; we shall fight on the landing grounds; we shall fight on the fields and in the streets; we shall fight in the hills; we shall never surrender."

British Prime Minister Winston Churchill, 1940

WILLS'S CIGARETTES

THE CIVILIAN RESPIRATOR—HOW TO ADJUST IT

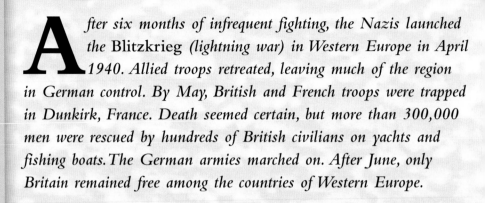

Afterter six months of infrequent fighting, the Nazis launched the **Blitzkrieg** *(lightning war) in Western Europe in April 1940. Allied troops retreated, leaving much of the region in German control. By May, British and French troops were trapped in Dunkirk, France. Death seemed certain, but more than 300,000 men were rescued by hundreds of British civilians on yachts and fishing boats. The German armies marched on. After June, only Britain remained free among the countries of Western Europe.*

A LIFE OF FEAR

In occupied countries in Western Europe, the Germans brought fear and chaos. German troops demanded respect, cooperation, and obedience. They took control over houses, offices, factories, transportation, and food supplies. The Germans forced European civilians to work in German-run factories and farms. They imposed strict nightly curfews. Anyone who protested was shot. Throughout Europe, living conditions were grim. Food and fuel were in short supply. Hospitals and schools could not function. People lost their jobs, their houses, their farms, and their families. By the end of 1940, there were more than 50 million refugees in Europe, searching for safety as the Germans advanced.

THE SEEDS OF GENOCIDE

Following Hitler's orders, thousands of men, women, and children with disabilities were considered "unfit." Some were sterilized or killed. Others were subjected to brutal experiments by Nazi doctors. Tall, blonde, blue-eyed women (whom the Nazis thought looked Aryan) were captured and handed over to German officers to breed more "ideal" Germans. Much of the groundwork for these practices had been laid in earlier Nazi practices.

In 1940, the seeds of genocide were firmly rooted when the death camp Auschwitz was built in Poland. The outlook for millions of civilians across Europe was about to become a nightmare of persecution, imprisonment, enslavement, torture, and death.

RESISTANCE

Some civilians decided that the only way to survive the Nazis was to collaborate with them. Most kept quiet, too

Below: British and French troops arrive safely in Dover, England, after being rescued from the Nazis off the coast of Dunkirk, France.

Above: *French Resistance fighters hide in a civilian apartment to take shots at German Nazi troops.*

TIME LINE 1939-1940

SEPTEMBER 27, 1939
British government raises taxes to pay for war.

NOVEMBER 12, 1939
Jews are banned from public places in Germany.

JANUARY 8, 1940
Food rationing begins in Britain.

APRIL – MAY, 1940
Following the invasion of Denmark, Norway, Netherlands, Belgium, Luxembourg, and France by Nazis, Neville Chamberlain resigns as British prime minister; Winston Churchill, a critic of Chamberlain's policy of "appeasement" with Hitler, takes his place in office.

JUNE 14, 1940
German death camp at Auschwitz, Poland, is opened.

JUNE 17, 1940
General Charles de Gaulle, leader of the Free French (anti-Nazis), escapes to Britain.

scared to question the changes that were taking place. A few men and women risked their lives to fight the Nazi invaders, however. Those people formed the groups known collectively as the Resistance. They smuggled weapons, planted bombs, cut phone and electricity cables, sabotaged factories, blew up trains, and shot at German soldiers. Resistance fighters spied on German troop movements, set up secret transmitters, forged vital documents, sent coded messages, and worked alongside secret agents from Allied countries. They sheltered soldiers trapped behind enemy lines, and they helped Jewish people escape to safety.

INTO THE U.S.S.R.

In 1939, Germany and the U.S.S.R. were at peace with each other. But in June 1941, Hitler ordered Nazi troops to invade Soviet land. As the Nazis advanced, Jews, Roma, and other minority groups were

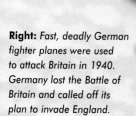

Right: *Fast, deadly German fighter planes were used to attack Britain in 1940. Germany lost the Battle of Britain and called off its plan to invade England.*

massacred. As German armies besieged Leningrad, Stalingrad, and Moscow, civilians became targeted for attack. Thousands of people were trapped in fear and horror.

The longest siege, at Leningrad, lasted from 1941 to 1944. Homes were destroyed by shells, and gunfire rang out in the streets. Soviet citizens shivered in rags, eating rats and grass to survive because they were forbidden by German troops from receiving food or fuel.

THE HOLOCAUST BEGINS

Before World War II, some German Jews managed to flee Germany. There were Jewish communities in other European nations, but some of those were also under attack as the Nazis ransacked Europe. The total number of Jews in Europe was relatively small—probably fewer than 10 million. Hitler was determined to eliminate all Jews, and Jewish civilians in Nazi-occupied lands were treated worst of all. By the time Germany had invaded their homelands, escape was impossible. The few Jews who managed to survive usually did so by hiding.

IN THE GHETTOS

In many German-occupied cities, Jewish families were confined like prisoners in crowded ghettoes. Those ghettoes were walled off from the rest of the city. Jews living there were denied basic food, medical, and social services. Thousands died of hunger, cold, or disease. As the war progressed, the campaign to exterminate Jews accelerated. The ghettoes became holding places where Jews were sent before being transported to death camps. Although they were aware of their uncertain fate,

> "Her whole body was buried under the sand but she did not move until it began to cover her mouth. She was lying face upwards, breathed in some sand and started to choke, and then, scarcely realizing what she was doing, she started to struggle in a state of uncontrollable panic....
>
> With her left hand, the good one [a Nazi soldier had crushed her other hand], she started scraping the sand off herself, scarcely daring to breathe lest she should start coughing; she used what strength she had to hold the cough back."
>
> **Martin Gilbert, author of The Holocaust, recounts the experience of Dina Pronicheva, a survivor of the Babi Yar massacre, where 30,000 Jews were killed in Kiev, Ukraine, 1941**

Right: *German-born Jewish teenager Anne Frank (1929–1945) escaped with her family to the Netherlands, then spent two years in hiding. Frank was eventually arrested and taken to a concentration camp, where she died. Her diary, found after her death, became a symbol of the strength of the human spirit under the worst conditions.*

Above: *Nazi soldiers arrest civilians in the Jewish ghetto in Warsaw, Poland. Between July and September 1942, the Nazis shipped about 265,000 Jews from Warsaw to the death camp Treblinka.*

ghetto dwellers tried to live normally. They set up schools, shared food, played music, and celebrated Jewish festivals. Many ordinary men and women showed extraordinary courage, such as Dr. Janus Korczak, who ran a home for Jewish orphans in the Warsaw Ghetto, Poland. Korczak chose to be killed beside the Jews rather than to abandon them.

NAZI MASSACRES

In Poland and the Baltic states of Estonia, Latvia, and Lithuania, Nazi *Einsatzgruppen* (task forces) traveled to each village. Those death squads looted Jewish homes and shot the inhabitants—often forcing them to dig their own graves beforehand. Around 1.5 million Jews were murdered in this brutal manner.

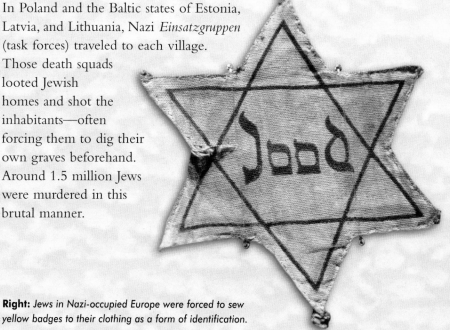

Right: *Jews in Nazi-occupied Europe were forced to sew yellow badges to their clothing as a form of identification.*

TIME LINE 1940

JUNE 28, 1940
All foreigners in the United States must be registered and fingerprinted.

JULY 10 – OCTOBER 31, 1940
In the Battle of Britain, German fighter planes attack England, but fail to conquer it. Churchill praised the bravery of British pilots killed fighting the invaders, "Never ... was so much owed by so many to so few."

"Because Leningrad's water system was destroyed, children went to the river and brought up water in buckets. In winter, thousands of 'ice children' dug up ice from the river to bring home to their family. Black market food soared to unbelievable prices. Two weeks' salary were required to buy a loaf of bread."

Grim conditions endured by civilians during the German siege of Leningrad (St. Petersburg), as described in an exhibition about Russian experiences in World War II

Above: Shocked civilians survey the charred ruins of a busy street after a German bombing raid on Coventry, England, in 1940.

Throughout the war, the Axis powers dropped bombs on military and civilian targets. Beginning in 1940, intensive bombing raids on British civilians began with the nightly blitz. More than 5,800 tons (5,262 tonnes) fell on London during the first month alone. The Germans aimed for Britain's national institutions, such as Parliament, and its shipping docks. However, bombs also hit places where civilians dwelled, such as houses, shops, and schools.

FIREBOMBS AND ROCKETS

Likewise, American, British, and other Allied nations bombed civilian targets in Germany and Japan, particularly toward the end of the war. The purpose of those bombings was not only military gain. The Allied powers also wanted to demoralize the Axis nations and make them believe their defeat was inevitable.

In 1940, Germany tried a new, deadly, weapon: firebombs. Nine hundred fell on the British city of Coventry on November 14. On that day, 550 civilians were killed and one-third of the houses in Coventry were destroyed. German bombers also dropped landmines on highly populated civilian areas. In 1944 and 1945, Germans launched unmanned V-1 bombs and V-2 rockets. They flew for a fixed distance and then fell and exploded without warning, killing random civilians.

ALLIED RAIDS

To retaliate, British and American bombers made equally damaging raids on German targets. The United States bombed by day, targeting German railways, bridges, and industrial centers. Britain bombed at night, striking densely populated cities sheltering troops and civilian refugees. In 1944, more than 130,000 people were killed when British planes firebombed Dresden, a city in northern Germany.

Right: A German V-2 rocket sits ready to launch in 1945. Rocket attacks were a terrifying form of warfare.

> "[London] was on fire. The Guildhall [historic trade center and mayor's office] was on fire. Wherever one looked up the narrow alleys of the city, you saw what looked like red snowstorms. Great showers of sparks were coming from the buildings…. I loved the city … and there I was, simply watching it burn."
>
> **Stanley Baron, a newspaper reporter, describes the London Blitz, 1940**

Above: A painting made during World War II shows fires caused by German bombing raids on London.

AFTER PEARL HARBOR

On December 7, 1941, an early morning Japanese bombing raid on the U.S. naval base at Pearl Harbor, Hawaii, killed and wounded more than 3,500 people. The attack caught U.S. forces by surprise, despite signs that Japan had been preparing for action against the United States for some time.

The bombing of Pearl Harbor pushed the United States to enter the war. Beginning in 1942, U.S. planes made strategic bombing raids on Japan. They used firebombs to devastate Tokyo, killing 100,000 civilians in a single raid. In August 1945, the United States dropped the world's first atomic bombs on two Japanese port cities, Hiroshima and Nagasaki. Approximately 150,000 people were killed in Hiroshima, many dying after the blast from radiation poisoning. In Nagasaki, about 40,000 people were killed instantly; others were left injured. Those attacks, in combination with the Soviet Union's invasion of Japanese-occupied Manchuria that same month, was too much for Japan. The war was over.

> "When I was rescued, my hair was burned; my face was inflated like a balloon…. It was hell. I saw people looking for water and they died soon after they drank it. I saw many people go to the river in search of water who died. The whole city was destroyed and burning. There was no place to go."
>
> **Michiko Yamaoka remembers the bombing of Hiroshima, Japan, 1945**

TIME LINE
1940-1941

SEPTEMBER 7, 1940
Start of the blitz aerial attacks on London.

FEBRUARY 4, 1941
United Service Organizations founded in United States.

FEBRUARY 16, 1941
Nazis deport 10,000 Jews from Vienna, Austria.

MARCH 1, 1941
U.S. Congress passes Lend-Lease Act to supply planes, ships, and weapons to Britain and the other Allied nations.

APRIL 6, 1941
Germans bomb Belgrade, Yugoslavia, in "Operation Punishment."

MAY 10, 1941
The end of the London blitz. Six months of bombing leaves 40,000 civilians killed and more than 80,000 injured.

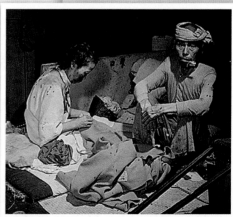

Right: Japanese medics help survivors of the atomic bombing of Hiroshima, Japan.

> "When bombs were falling, I have seen big men become rooted to the spot, transfixed by terror beyond their control. I have seen others set off and run blindly in sheer panic, in no particular direction...."

Hugh Varah, British firefighter during World War II

Below: *An Air Raid Precaution warden cradles a homeless child in her arms following the bombing by Nazi troops of Norwich, England.*

SHATTERED LIVES

During the London blitz, newspapers and posters published defiant slogans such as, "Britain can take it!" In reality, bombing raids took a terrible toll on England. Thousands of civilians died from blast injuries, fires, and suffocation. Countless more were injured or disabled.

Families were immediately traumatized by explosions, and later by homelessness, hunger, the loss of possessions, and the breakdown of normal life. The loss of family pets, many of which had run away in fear, added to the misery of those who had already lost so much, especially children. People in bombed cities became depressed and prone to panic attacks. Some developed strange behaviors or fell physically ill from stress. Weeks of sleepless nights left people short-tempered, forgetful, and exhausted.

Above: *A German fire-bomb is pictured on a British government warning poster in 1940.*

CIVILIAN HELPERS

At the same time, civilians made tremendous efforts to help survivors and limit the damage done by bombing raids. British Air Raid Precautions wardens walked the streets, checking air-raid shelters and rescuing people from collapsed buildings. They joined teams of firefighters or the new Auxiliary Fire Service. Women worked at telephone switchboards, as messengers, despatch riders, ambulance drivers, and first-aid medics. They ran emergency shelters that offered food, clothes, blankets, and a place to rest for victims and emergency crews.

BLACKOUTS

Civilians in many European countries, and even Americans living in the northeastern United States, had to obey strict electricity regulations. Streetlights were switched off, windows were fitted with heavy curtains, and train lighting was dimmed to stop escaping light from guiding German bombers.

BRUTAL INVADERS

Many European, Soviet, and Asian civilians risked their lives during everyday activities, such as buying food. Troops fought their way along streets, shooting windows and smashing doors to hunt for enemy soldiers, while frightened men, women, and children cowered in basements or inner rooms. Invading armies brutally attacked citizens. In 1937, Japan invaded Nanking, China, killing more than 300,000 civilians. In 1944, when Japan entered the Philippines, all males over age 14 in Manila were shot. In 1945, Soviet soldiers killed thousands of German civilians. Those actions were taken in revenge for atrocities that the Nazis had committed against Soviet civilians.

> "I didn't usually worry about air raids, but once I was cycling home to London after a trip to the countryside. I reached the top of a hill, and saw London spread out before me. I could also see planes overhead, and searchlights, and hear anti-aircraft gunfire. I felt sure that my home would be hit by a bomb, and raced the last miles home in a panic. The nearer I got, the more certain I felt that I would find my family dead and our house in ruins!"
>
> **Geoff Field, an 11-year-old boy, remembers bombing raids in London**

TIME LINE 1941

MAY 27, 1941
U.S. President Roosevelt declares a national emergency; urges all Americans to oppose Nazism.

DECEMBER 7, 1941
Japan attacks U.S. naval base at Pearl Harbor, Hawaii, killing or injuring more than 3,500.

DECEMBER 8 – 11, 1941
United States first declares war on Japan, followed by Germany and Italy.

DECEMBER 1941
In strikes that last for more than a year, Japan occupies Guam, Hong Kong, the Philippines, Thailand, Malaya, Singapore, Java, Borneo, Bali, Sumatra, Timor, and Burma. Civilians are imprisoned, forced into labor camps, and starved.

Above: *Civilians spend the night underground, sheltered from German bombing raids in a London subway station in 1940.*

> "I never felt scared in the blackout. I was only 18 but I left my workplace in total darkness, walked alone though unlighted city streets, and caught a dark train back to my village. Anyone could have followed me or sat next to me; you just couldn't see people's faces . . . . In winter, the [steam] trains were bitterly cold, as well as dark. There was barely enough coal for their fuel, and none for heating. I used to take a hot water bottle with me...."
>
> **Mary Mills, a 16-year-old working girl from southern England, recalls the WWII blackouts**

Above: *A long line outside the passport office in London. Many people tried to evacuate to Canada during World War II.*

SEEKING SAFETY

To escape the war, children, pregnant women, and nursing mothers were often evacuated from cities to the country. That was possible only before Nazi invaders had taken control; after that, few citizens could travel freely. Even before the war began, many families made arrangements to stay with friends or relatives who lived in the country. Wealthy European parents sent their children far away, to South Africa, Australia, Canada, or the United States.

Left: *In this photo, a teacher drives her class of evacuated children back to the farms where they are staying.*

In Britain, the government organized an official evacuation. From 1939, children from cities were assembled, labeled with their names and ages, and put on special trains or buses supervised by female volunteers. At their destinations, they were handed over to volunteer host families.

AWAY FROM HOME

The contrasts between urban and rural life were often difficult for both the city children and their rural hosts. Misunderstandings were common; hosts and evacuees spoke in different accents and dialects. Some city children faced prejudices.

Many hosts also had different expectations of behavior, manners, and hygiene. Understandably, many children missed their parents and were homesick. Others settled into daily routines and formed lasting friendships.

Back in the cities, some parents worried about their children so much that they brought them home again, against government advice. Those parents preferred to risk dying as a family, rather than be separated. They found it easier to endure the hardships of life on the home front when surrounded by loved ones.

Below: *Children play in Dover, England, in 1941. That area came to be known as "Hellfire Corner" because it faced heavy bombing raids by Nazi troops.*

TIME LINE 1942

JANUARY 17, 1942
Nazi leaders announce the "Final Solution," a plan to kill all European Jews.

FEBRUARY 23, 1942
Mutual Aid Agreement is signed; the United States provides warships and weapons for Britain.

FEBRUARY 23, 1942
Japanese submarine bombs a U.S. oil field in California.

MARCH, 1942
British planes bomb German Baltic Sea ports.

APRIL 1942
U.S. planes bomb Japan; Japanese massacre 250,000 Chinese in retaliation for the country's support of the United States.

"When I got to school, there was no morning prayers and we were given a badge to wear with a number. We were told to sit in class, everyone looking at each other but no one told us anything. We were being evacuated. We were billeted [housed] with a family in a little village in Wales. I'd never been to the country before."

Derek Haycock remembers being evacuated to Wales as a child, 1939

"you buy 'em
we'll fly 'em!"

DEFENSE
BONDS
STAMPS

Above: *A patriotic U.S. airman encourages Americans to buy war bonds to support U.S. troops during World War II.*

In all countries fighting in World War II, civilians' lives were disrupted, even if their city or town had not been invaded or bombed. All civilians were expected to take part in their nation's war effort by making personal sacrifices.

THE WAR EFFORT

In the United States, people cut back on wearing fashionable clothing and shoes due to the rationing of cloth and other materials, such as rubber. Silk was among the limited materials, leading to the wartime invention of nylons as a replacement for silk stockings. To make due, people patched clothing and children wore items handed down from older siblings. People were also urged to save cooking fat or oil drippings, put them in tin cans, and then sell or donate the fat to be used to make explosives for bombs.

World leaders reorganized national economies, controlling prices to stop traders from making unfair profits from rationed goods. The U.S. government collected higher taxes to pay for troops and weapons and raised additional money for the war by selling war bonds.

"I worked the graveyard shift 12:00–8:00 A.M. in the shipyard. I took classes on how to weld. I had leather gloves, pants, a big hood, goggles, and a leather jacket . . . . They put me 40 feet down in the bottom of the ship to be a tacker. I filled the long seams of the cracks in the ship corners full of hot lead and then brushed them good and you could see how pretty it was. The welders would come along and weld it so it would take the strong waves and deep water and heavy weight. I liked it pretty good.

I don't remember how much I got paid for working. Lots of people came to Richmond, [Virginia], to work in the shipyards. I told Melvin [her husband, fighting overseas] that I helped to make a ship for him to come home in."

Katie Grant, a young, married woman, describing the skills she learned in U.S. shipyards, making and repairing warships

Below: *Women contribute to the war effort by driving tanks, trucks, and testing guns for the U.S. Army.*

WAR INDUSTRIES

Everywhere, industry was transformed. Factories were converted to make tanks, planes, warships, gas masks, and uniforms, rather than athletic equipment, cosmetics, or clothing. Civilian workers were ordered to stop making consumer goods, such as stoves and cars, and to start making weapons. Everyone was encouraged to grow their own fruits and vegetables and save 10 percent of their earnings.

New mass-production methods, such as assembly lines pioneered by Henry Ford in the United States and Friedrich Krupp in Germany, were used in wartime factories. Those new methods enabled factories to make vast quantities of identical items such as bullets. Entire industries emerged around manufacturing clothing and other items that might otherwise not have been in such demand. The U.S. Army ordered more than 4 million rifles, for example, and 57 million soldiers' uniforms. Because raw materials for industry were so scarce, scientists invented synthetic replacements, such as a new form of rubber. They also found new uses for everyday products. For instance, peanut oil was used to lubricate heavy machines.

WOMEN LEND A HAND

In the United States, women's branches of the armed forces were set up by the Army and Navy. Women piloted aircraft to deliver goods and supplies. None of those roles had before been open to women. An increasing number of men were serving—and dying—in the war, so women stepped in to manufacture and deliver war supplies.

Right: *A woman works on the assembly line at an ammunition factory in California.*

> "It was a big place. My guess would be that some 30,000 workers were running three shifts and that they were making a very presentable number of airplanes each day....
>
> More than 35 percent of the labor in the plant was done by women. Among the workers we saw boys not more than ten years old … the children work, in many of the [factory departments], the full sixty-hour week worked by adults."
>
> **U.S. business and political leader Wendell Wilkie, 1940**

TIME LINE
1942

APRIL 23, 1942
German planes bomb British cities famous for their old buildings in *Baedecker* ("Tourist") raids.

APRIL 28, 1942
The northeastern United States practices "dim-outs" to protect against approaching German bombers and submarines.

MAY 15, 1942
Fuel rationing begins in the United States.

MAY 18, 1942
German protesters are shot while putting up anti-Nazi posters in Berlin, Germany.

MAY 30, 1942
Britain begins massive bombing raids on German cities.

FOOD IS A WEAPON

DON'T WASTE IT!
BUY WISELY - COOK CAREFULLY - EAT IT ALL

FOLLOW THE NATIONAL WARTIME NUTRITION PROGRAM

Above: *In all war-torn countries, governments urged civilians not to waste food.*

A FAIR SHARE

As well as controlling the placement of workers, governments everywhere mandated rationing. Rationing limited the quantity of food, clothing, fuel, and other essential items that each person could buy. Rationing rules applied to everyone, rich or poor. Government officials wanted to allow a equal share of items and materials that were in short supply because they were needed for the war. Some goods were scarce because the raw materials used to make them—such as red meat, cotton, or oil—were being redirected to feed, clothe, and transport troops and equipment in the war. Other goods, such as cars, were limited because the factories making them were being used to manufacture ammunition, tanks, and other military equipment. Citizens had to prove their right to receive rationed goods. Governments issued each citizen with a ration book and coupons. Customers handed those over with cash when making a purchase. Buying rationed items without coupons was prohibited.

RATIONING FUEL

Coal and gasoline rationing saved energy to power factories, warships, and planes. Oil and gas were needed to transport troops and weapons, and to provide heating, lighting, and hot water

"To save gasoline, tires, and vehicles, . . . Connecticut has a reduced the maximum speed limit to 40 miles per hour (mph). The former top speed was 50 mph on main routes. The State's action is [likely] the forerunner of a nation-wide trend that will serve both safety and economy when both are needed in a time of war."

***The New York Times,
January, 1942***

Below: *A photograph taken during World War II shows children eating naturally sweet carrots, instead of sugary treats that were unavailable in wartime.*

Above: *Women in London wait in a long line, hoping to buy potatoes, which although not rationed, were often in short supply during the war.*

TIME LINE
1942

MAY 1942
The Women's Army Corps is established as a branch of the U.S. Army.

JUNE 7, 1942
U.S. Navy wins the Battle of Midway against Japan.

JULY 1942
WAVES (Women Accepted for Voluntary Emergency Services) is set up as a branch of the U.S. Navy.

AUGUST – SEPT. 1942
Japanese planes drop bombs on U.S. forests in Oregon.

for civilians. Families often drew lines around bathtubs, 5 inches (12.5 centimeters) above the bottom, to avoid wasting water.

PRECIOUS FOOD

Imported foods were no longer available in many countries, so people learned to cook with substitutes. Leftovers might be fed to food-producing animals, such as chickens. Or they might be collected by members of "Pig-Clubs," who raised and fattened a pig and then shared its meat between them.

In occupied countries, and also in Germany, people often went hungry and sometimes starved. In the Netherlands, there was a dreadful famine in the winter of 1944–1945. Desperate citizens tried to survive by eating daffodil and tulip bulbs.

WAR FASHIONS

Wartime clothes, hats, shoes, house furnishings, and even children's toys were also

Below: *A U.S. wartime ration book is shown alongside ration stamps.*

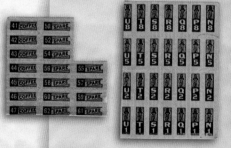

"The U.S. government has taken several important steps to eliminate unjustified increases in prices and to assure everyone a fair share of food. Many essential foods have been rationed. Legal prices have been established on practically every food item. Your government is counting on you to help enforce the new regulations by making and keeping this simple pledge: I will accept no rationed foods without giving ration stamps. I will never pay more than legal prices."

A U.S. War Rations Notice, 1941

> "I had no ration coupons to buy little shoes for my bridesmaids, so I made them myself out of left-over scraps of cloth with cardboard for the soles."
>
> **Jane Smith, a British wartime bride, recalling how she planned for her wedding day despite cloth rationing**

affected by rationing. In the United States, clothes styles were simple and fitted closely, so as not to waste precious material. Many designs featured square shoulders and belted waists, like army jackets. Shoes were sturdy and designed to be long-lasting rather than fashionable. Socks and women's stockings made of fine wool, silk, or cotton were scarce. Instead, many women wore trousers (a new, daring fashion) or siren suits. (Those were all-in-one jumpsuits, warm and cozy in drafty air raid shelters.) For special occasions, young women covered their legs with tinted cream, although such cosmetics and perfume were expensive luxuries. At work, women tied their hair back under nets or scarves. For parties, they tried styles with patriotic names like the "Victory Roll." Short hair, or the American crew cut, were in style for men.

During the war, new clothes or shoes were rare. Everyone tried to "Make Do and Mend," by sewing and patching existing items. Dresses and trousers were repaired, and sweaters were knitted from scrap wool. Hats (worn by most people in the 1940s) were often homemade using wild bird's feathers for decoration. Children wore clothing made from cut-down adult garments; babies were dressed in castoffs or kept warm in old blankets. Toys were homemade and often had a wartime theme: model soldiers, planes, guns, dolls dressed as nurses, or teddy bears made from scrap fabrics. Older children liked to play in ruined and bombed buildings, although dangers from unstable structures and unexploded munitions made that a very dangerous pastime.

LIFE DURING WARTIME

Families whose homes had been bombed needed to find new furnishings. Wood was in short supply (it was used for building ships and planes), as were fabrics. Many families in war-torn Europe had to wait for replacements until long after the end of the war. In Britain, however, the government allowed limited quantities of basic household items to be made in plain styles.

DIG FOR VICTORY

Civilians grumbled about wartime regulations, but they also worked hard for the war effort. In the United States and in Britain, people grew fruit and vegetables in backyard "victory gardens," and they kept chickens, rabbits, and goats for eggs, meat, and milk. In the United States, an estimated 20 million backyard gardens produced about 40 percent of the nation's fruit and vegetables.

Below: A British propaganda poster promotes sewing as an essential skill in wartime. Even troops were taught to mend holes in their socks.

MAKE-DO AND MEND says Mrs. Sew-and-Sew

Left: *During the war, British women spun hair combed from their dogs to make yarn, which they then knit into warm gloves, socks, and scarves.*

TIME LINE
1942-1944

SEPT. 1942 – FEB. 1943
Germans bomb Stalingrad, U.S.S.R. Half a million citizens die; the survivors refuse to surrender.

DECEMBER 1, 1942
Beveridge Report is published in Britain. It plans a new "Welfare State" for civilians.

JANUARY 28, 1943
All German adults are mobilized for "total war."

APRIL 19, 1943
Jews in the Warsaw Ghetto rise up.

SEPTEMBER 3, 1943
Italy agrees to secret peace treaty with Britain, United States, and the other Allies.

APRIL 1943 – JUNE 1944
Some 16,000 captured Allied troops and 80,000 Asian civilians die building Burma-Thailand railway for Japanese.

JULY 27, 1943
Britain bombs Hamburg, Germany; 40,000 civilians die.

JANUARY 6, 1944
Soviet troops advance into German-occupied Poland.

JUNE 6, 1944
British, American, and other Allied forces start D-Day invasion to recapture German-occupied France.

Those measures helped people save money. They became more self-reliant. That was critical for Britain, where attacks on ships bringing in food from other parts of the world were often attacked by German U–boats.

SURVIVAL STRATEGIES

To help people adjust to rationing food, the U.S. government sponsored training sessions to teach citizens how to shop wisely. The classes taught how to plan meals with set limitations, such as including less red meat. Wild foods also helped keep many civilians alive, especially in the U.S.S.R., Poland, and eastern Germany. People whose homes or farms had been destroyed were forced to scavenge in fields and forests for nettles, nuts, and berries. In autumn, they gathered mushrooms and acorns. In Britain, government factories processed wild rose-hips, picked by civilian volunteers, to extract life-saving vitamin C.

Left: *A woman is dressed in a blouse and overalls, which cost very few ration stamps.*

RECYCLING

In the United States, schools, neighorhoods, and places of worship organized scrap drives. Those efforts helped collect different kinds of waste materials for recycling to help with the war effort. Metal toothpaste tubes, cooking pots, gates, and fences were melted and turned into planes and warships. Old paper was turned into aircraft engine gaskets and packaging for gun cartridges. Almost all used materials were put to good use. If they were not directly used for the war, they were repurposed for personal use.

Above: *Children in Washington, D.C., collect scrap metal for the war effort.*

HOME COMFORTS

Civilians also helped by renting rooms to war–factory workers, walking to work, sharing cars to save gasoline, and donating blood. Americans, Canadians, Australians, and others living in lands that had not been invaded, showed great kindness and generosity and packed "Bundles for Britain"—parcels full of practical and luxury items. Many women knitted warm socks and scarves for the troops, and families invited refugees into their homes. Wives, children, parents, and neighbors wrote letters to cheer and comfort troops serving far from home.

Below: *As well as sending letters to comfort troops overseas, generous civilians on the home front also gave money to charities that sent food parcels to Allied prisoners-of-war.*

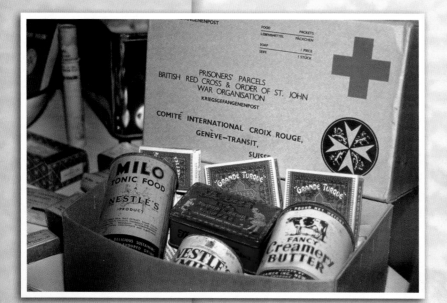

Left: *A World War II-era poster encourages people to care for their gardens.*

Below: *A U.S. Navy sailor is delighted to receive a letter from home.*

TIME LINE
1944

JUNE 6, 1944
British, American, and other Allied forces start D-Day invasion.

JUNE 12, 1944
German troops target British cities with V-1 bombs.

AUGUST 25, 1944
German troops retreat from Paris.

SEPTEMBER 8, 1944
German troops send powerful V-2 rockets to attack Britain.

OCTOBER 25, 1944
U.S. Navy destroys Japanese fleet at the Battle of Leyte Gulf.

COMMUNITY SPIRIT

For people on the home front in the United States and Britain, winning the war was considered a way of life. Along with personal sacrifices, frequent air raid drills, and the breakup of families, came patriotism and a strengthened sense of community.

The civilian war effort was essential. Without it, governments, military personnel, and civilians would not have survived. Life during the war was tough for women, especially if they were married. They worked long hours, cared for children, and managed their homes. In addition, many women did voluntary work. At the same time, many lived with the fear of wondering whether their husbands, sons, and brothers would safely return from the war.

Above: *During the war, Americans enjoyed epic romances, such as* Gone with the Wind. *People looked forward to forgetting their worries for a while.*

C ivilians on the home front faced bombing raids, rationing, curfews, blackouts, supply shortages, extended working hours, travel difficulties, and absent loved ones. In the United States, everyone looked forward to an occasional night out with friends. It was a chance for people to enjoy themselves and forget the nightmares of war for a while.

BIG BAND ERA

In the United States, big bands were led by instrumentalists, such as Glenn Miller and Tommy Dorsey. During the war, ballroom dancing was among the most popular forms of entertainment. Many people met their future wives or husbands at a dance. In rural areas, energetic traditional dances were just as popular.

In between dances, glamorous solo singers, such as Frank Sinatra or Helen Forrest, might croon a romantic ballad or sing of a future without war. Among the most well-known singers were Britain's Vera Lynn, "the Forces Sweetheart," and German-born actress Marlene Dietrich, who lived and worked in the United States. Her songs were popular with Allied and Axis troops alike.

AT THE MOVIES

Cinema was also extremely popular during the war. In Allied countries, films ranged from newsreels of important events, to cartoons featuring Disney's Mickey Mouse

"On Saturday nights, we all liked to go dancing. We girls changed out of our working clothes and put on a dress, if we had one. Many of the men were in uniform. The dances were great fun, but also rather sad. When you said good-bye at the end of the evening, you could never be sure that you would see your dancing partners again. By next Saturday, they might have been killed in action...."

Mary Jones, a teenage girl living in Britain during WWII

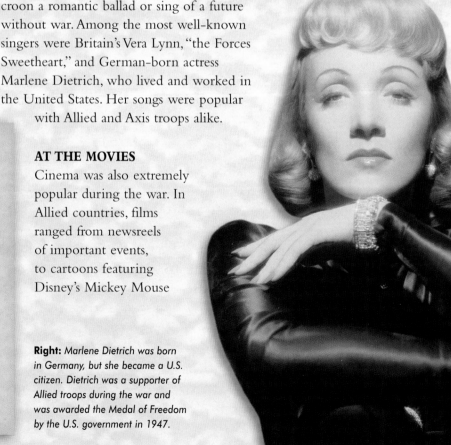

Right: *Marlene Dietrich was born in Germany, but she became a U.S. citizen. Dietrich was a supporter of Allied troops during the war and was awarded the Medal of Freedom by the U.S. government in 1947.*

Above: U.S. servicemen dance at London's Rainbow Club in 1945, a popular club for Americans stationed in Britain during World War II.

TIME LINE
1944-1945

DECEMBER 3, 1944
British Home Guard told to stand down from duties.

JANUARY 27, 1945
Soviet troops liberate Auschwitz concentration camp in Poland.

Below: In this film poster, Charlie Chaplin, dressed as Hitler, pokes fun at the German dictator in the film The Great Dictator.

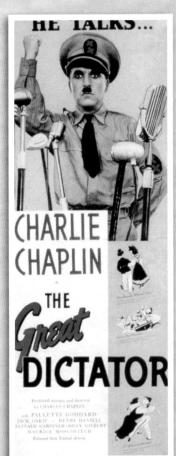

in uniform. Heroic dramas, such as *Destination Tokyo* (1943) and *In Which We Serve* (1942), matched the mood of the period. There were also passionate romances such as *Gone With the Wind* (1939), and chronicles of civilian life, such as *Since You Went Away* (1944), which helped people escape from or cope with the day-to-day drama of life on the home front.

Some Hollywood movies boldly satirized Hitler and Nazi Germany and, to a lesser extent, Japan, even before the Japanese attacked Pearl Harbor in 1941. Top comedian Charlie Chaplin brilliantly ridiculed Hitler in the feature-length film *The Great Dictator* (1940). That film was preceded by a lesser-known short film featuring the Three Stooges called *You Nazty Spy* (1940), in which actor Moe Howard did the first cinematic impression of Hitler. The Three Stooges (all of whom were Jewish and aware of the Nazis' persecution of European Jews) followed this film with a sequel called *I'll Never Heil Again* (1941).

Above: In 1938, a British family holds gas masks while listening anxiously to the radio for news of Hitler's threats.

HELP FROM THE STARS

Many famous performers, such as Bob Hope, volunteered to entertain servicemen and women. In Britain, government appointed ENSA entertainers (affectionately nicknamed "Every Night Something Awful") who toured troop camps in dangerous war zones. Some stars used their fame to speak out against Hitler. Among them was British actor Leslie Howard, who died when his plane was shot down by German aircraft in 1943.

OVER THE AIRWAVES

In the 1940s, television sets were rare in the United States. In Britain, television was shut down in 1939 at the start of the war. Even without television, however, access to information could be had by listening to the radio. Broadcasting played a vital part in the war effort in every country, uniting listeners and giving them important news updates. Government leaders appeared on radio regularly. U.S. President Roosevelt and British Prime Minister Winston Churchill became famous for their inspiring speeches. Radio stations also broadcast brisk, cheerful songs from the era of swing music. Light-hearted programs featured favorite comedians, such as Jack Benny, George Burns and Gracie Allen, Bing Crosby, and Groucho Marx.

> "We would listen to the radio every night. One particular Sunday night the Germans sunk the *Wales* and the *Repulse,* which were British ships. When you're listening to it on the radio, ... it's very profound to think that this is actually happening somewhere in the world and you're sitting safe in your house."
>
> **Katherine O'Grady, an American wartime radio listener**

Left: British journalist Sefton Delmer (1904–1979) is broadcasting false information to Germany in 1941. Some propaganda aimed to comfort civilians; some was designed to mislead enemies.

TRUTH AND LIES

Wartime radio reporters sent back the first live accounts of the war. Listeners were deeply moved. Most news bulletins were carefully censored. Only limited information was released, to avoid panic and reduce the risk of revealing useful information to enemies. Some broadcasts were in code and contained messages to secret agents operating in enemy territory. Others were designed to deceive. British traitor William Joyce ("Lord Haw Haw") spoke from Germany, urging British civilians to surrender. Japanese-American "Tokyo Rose" made demoralizing broadcasts to U.S. troops.

Above: Wartime propaganda posters warned against discussing troop movements to avoid giving enemies any advantages.

PROPAGANDA

Everywhere, governments used propaganda (messages with the intent to persuade) to encourage, inform, and command civilians. Propaganda appeared in several formats: radio broadcasts, newspaper articles, films, and brightly colored posters. All featured wartime role models: heroic troops, thrifty housewives, hard-working women, factory workers, and brave firefighters. Governments hoped that those images would inspire civilians to work harder. Governments also published useful information, such as how to build a bomb shelter or stay safe during a poison gas attack.

Commercial companies liked to include propaganda slogans in their advertisements. They hoped that by linking their products to patriotic themes they would win more customers. Advertisements and propaganda often used humor to get their message across.

TIME LINE 1945

FEBRUARY 11, 1945
U.S. President Roosevelt, Soviet Premier Stalin, and Britian's Prime Minister Churchill meet at Yalta, Ukraine, to plan the final attack on the Nazis.

FEBRUARY 13 – 14, 1945
British and U.S. planes bomb Dresden, Germany.

MARCH 9, 1945
U.S. planes firebomb Tokyo, Japan.

MARCH 27 – 29, 1945
Last V-1 and V-2 rocket attacks on London are launched by Germany.

"When der fuehrer says we is de master race,

We heil . . . heil . . . right in der fuehrer's face.

Not to love der fuehrer is a great disgrace,

So we heil . . . heil . . . right in der fuehrer's face.

When Herr Goebbels says we own the world and space,

We heil . . . heil . . . right in Herr Goebbels' face.

When Herr Goering says they'll never bomb dis place,

We heil . . . heil . . . right in Herr Goring's face."

"Der Fuehrer's Face," Spike Jones, 1943, the theme to Disney's anti-Nazi propaganda cartoon of the same name

"In 1943, I arrived in Tehran in Persia [Iran] on a train from Siberia with thousands of other children, ... No mothers. No fathers. No adults except for the soldiers.

We were all put into hostels until we could be claimed by someone, or adopted. I didn't speak much but I seemed to be Polish, and so when I was unclaimed the Polish Consul-General and his wife took me and called me 'Magdalena' and I became their daughter."

Magdalena Mokrzycki, one of millions of wartime refugees

World War II spread devastation around the world on a scale never before known. The conflict left the cities of many nations in ruins. Farms lay abandoned, businesses ceased to operate; governments had massive debts, and national economies were in crisis. At the same time, more than 100 million refugees were left struggling to survive with too little food and fuel and inadequate shelter. How could the hungry and homeless be looked after? How could peoples' lives return to normal after years of struggle?

EMERGENCY AID

International charities, such as the Red Cross, the Red Crescent, and the newly founded Oxfam, worked with civilian volunteers to assist refugees. Allied troops, thousands still stationed in Western Europe, also assisted refugees, but more help was needed.

Right: Red Cross nurses and other voluntary aid workers worked heroically to care for refugees after the war.

To bridge the gap, the United States gave nearly 14 billion dollars in goods and money toward rebuilding Europe, beginning in 1948. That pledge became known as the Marshall Plan, after the U.S. general who managed it. The Marshall Plan was generous, but it was also designed to win support for U.S. policies. It was rejected by the Soviet Union, which did not accept its terms.

A NEW BRITAIN

Postwar governments also made ambitious plans. In Britain, the new socialist government nationalized transportation systems and established welfare programs to rid the nation of "want, disease, ignorance, squalor, and idleness." From 1945, medical care and schooling were free, pensions were introduced, the unemployed got state aid, and mothers were given money to help raise healthier children.

THE IRON CURTAIN

Politically, there were still serious divisions. Two former wartime allies—the communist Soviet Union and the capitalist United States—were now bitter rivals. Both countries emerged from the war as superpowers with their own alliances. Soviet Premier Joseph Stalin had taken control of many Eastern European lands. In 1946, Churchill famously described the creation of the Soviet bloc nations as an "iron curtain" dividing Europe. Churchill voiced concern about the spread of communism in those regions. He said, "Communist parties ... are seeking everywhere to obtain totalitarian control." That iron curtain of communism would not rise until the early 1990s. That was when the Soviet Union broke apart into Russia and other independent republics.

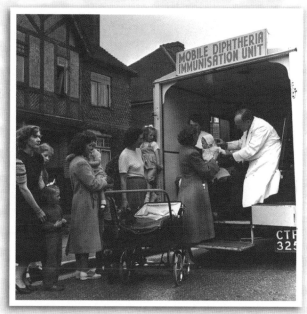

Above: *In Britain, the new National Health Service launched free mobile mass immunization services to combat dangerous infectious diseases, such as diphtheria.*

"The United States should do whatever it is able to do to assist in the return of normal economic health in the world, without which there can be no political stability and no assured peace. Our policy is directed not against any country or doctrine but against hunger, poverty, desperation, and chaos. Its purpose should be the revival of a working economy in the world so as to permit the emergence of political and social conditions in which free institutions can exist."

U.S. General George Marshall outlines the Marshall Plan, 1947

TIME LINE 1945

APRIL 24, 1945
Soviet troops surround Berlin, Germany.

APRIL 30, 1945
Hitler commits suicide.

MAY 7, 1945
Germany surrenders.

MAY 8, 1945
VE (Victory in Europe) Day is declared.

JUNE 26, 1945
United Nations is formed.

JULY 26, 1945
Churchill is replaced as Prime Minister by Clement Attlee.

AUGUST 6 – 9, 1945
United States drops atomic bombs on the Japanese cities of Hiroshima and Nagasaki.

AUGUST 8, 1945
U.S.S.R. attacks Japanese-occupied Manchuria; 500,000 civilians die.

AUGUST 14, 1945
Japan surrenders.

AUGUST 15, 1945
VJ (Victory over Japan) Day is declared.

AUGUST 16, 1945
Gas rationing ends in the United States.

Left: *In this photo, taken in New York City in 1945, a U.S. sailor and civilian nurse celebrate Japan's surrender to Allied forces. Above: A ship carrying soldiers from the U.S. 86th Infantry Division docks at New York Harbor in 1945.*

"To girls brought up on the cinema, who copied the dress, hair styles, and manners of Hollywood film stars, the sudden influx of Americans speaking like the films, who actually lived in the magic country, and who had plenty of money, at once went to the girls' heads. The Americans' proneness to spoil a girl, to build up, exaggerate, talk big and act with generosity and flamboyance, helped to make them the most attractive of boyfriends."

British government report, 1945

PACTS AND POWER

In the Middle East, Zionists (Jewish nationalists) and Jewish wartime survivors were struggling to set up a new nation, Israel, in a region that was dominated by Arab and other Muslim countries. In Asia, colonies ruled by European nations demanded independence. There were power struggles in China, and the divide between communists (backed by the Soviet Union and China) and capitalists (backed by the United States) was threatening peace and stability on the Korean Peninsula. With new rivalries rising to the surface after the threat of Nazism had been laid to rest, could another war be prevented?

ALL TOGETHER

Supported by the Allies, a promising new organization, the United Nations, was founded in 1945. Representatives from its member nations endorsed the Atlantic Charter, agreeing to use their resources to defend Allied powers. They hoped that future wars could be avoided by diplomacy and communication. In 1949, many countries also made alliances with the United States and the Soviet Union for security. In Western Europe, many nations joined the North Atlantic Treaty Organization (NATO), led by the Unites States. In Eastern Europe—under communist rule—countries joined the Council for Mutual Economic Assistance (COMECON) and the Warsaw Pact, both led by the Soviet Union.

Right: *The Security Council chamber is inside the United Nations in New York. Founded after World War II, the council's function is to maintain international peace.*

AN EMOTIONAL TIME

For most civilians, the end of World War II brought joy. In Allied countries, celebrating crowds thronged the streets; neighborhoods held victory parties. Troops liberating towns and cities from German occupation were welcomed as were returning servicemen, home safely at last.

However, many families faced a future without husbands and fathers. Many couples, after six years apart, also found it hard to adjust. More happily, many babies were born after 1945. Those children were soon called the "baby boom" generation. Thousands of G.I. brides (European women married to U.S. troops) started a new life in the United States.

Women who had worked in well-paid positions in the United States during the war, found themselves out of work. Employers preferred to hire returning servicemen. There were fewer peacetime jobs open to women, and many of those jobs paid poorly. Industries, advertisers, and the media promoted a new female image. Her task was to stay at home, keep after the house, shop for consumer goods, and care for children and men.

TOUGH TIMES

Even with aid from the Marshall Plan, it took years for European nations to recover. In the years just after the war, rationing continued, and some foods became scarcer. Clothing and furnishings were still drab, particularly in the Soviet-bloc nations. Families still shared cramped lodgings with relatives or friends. To make matters worse, the European winter of 1946 and 1947 was extremely harsh. Some refugees still faced starvation. That period became known as "the years of austerity."

LOOKING AHEAD

Slowly, businesses, industries, and public services began to recover. Governments invited men from Africa, Asia, and the Caribbean to come to Europe to work in new enterprises. France and Germany planned a new "Common Market" (now the European Community). They wanted the nations of Europe to grow prosperous together, without conflict. World War II was over and a new future was on the horizon.

TIME LINE
1945-1948

NOVEMBER 20, 1945
Surviving Nazi leaders are tried for war crimes in Nuremberg, Germany.

NOVEMBER 23, 1945
Food rationing ends in the United States.

JUNE 7, 1946
Television broadcasts begin again in Britain.

JULY 21, 1946
Bread rationing begins in Britain.

JUNE 22, 1948
Post-war immigrant workers come to Britain from the Caribbean.

Below: *In 1948, the Empire Windrush arrives at Tilbury docks in Britain with 500 Jamaican workers.*

World War II engulfed entire continents. It represented one of the clearest conflicts between forces of evil—the Axis nations led by Hitler's Nazi Germany—and those that would put a stop to that evil—the Allies, led by Britain and the United States. Despite the global nature of the conflict, it was fought not only in the trenches and skies of Europe and the Pacific, but in neighborhoods as ordinary people helped each other survive.

RAOUL WALLENBERG (1912 – 1947)

Swedish diplomat and businessman Raoul Wallenberg was sent to work in Hungary, an ally of Nazi Germany. He used his diplomatic status to help almost 100,000 Jewish people escape to safety, by issuing documents—which he created himself—giving them permission to travel. He also set up safe houses within Hungary, where Jewish people could shelter. He flew Swedish flags outside these refuges, and claimed they were Swedish territory. In 1945, Wallenberg was arrested by Soviet soldiers, advancing into Hungary. They accused him of being a spy. He was never seen again. Later, the Soviet government claimed he died in a Moscow prison, although many believe he may have lived for decades following his arrest.

MORDECAI ANIELEWICZ (1919 – 1943)

Polish-Jewish student Mordecai Anielewicz was born to a poor family. After leaving school, he joined a Jewish youth movement and proved himself to be an inspiring leader and organizer. Still a teenager, he tried to help Jews escape from Poland to Israel, but he was caught and put in prison. Once free, he returned to Warsaw, Poland, to join resistance fighters. In 1943, he learned that the Nazis planned to shut down the Warsaw Ghetto and send all its inhabitants to concentration camps. The Jews in the ghetto were outnumbered by Nazi troops, and they had no chance of surviving, but they battled bravely for four weeks, led by Anielewicz. They refused to surrender even after he was killed.

JEAN MOULIN (1899 – 1943)

French government official Jean Moulin refused to obey orders from Nazis in occupied France. In 1940, after being dismissed from his job, he joined the French Resistance. He spent the rest of his life in disguise and on the run. In 1943, Moulin made a secret journey to Britain, where General Charles de Gaulle, leader of the exiled Free French forces, trusted him with a mission to organize the resistance groups. Shortly after setting up the National Council of the Resistance in 1943, Moulin was captured by the Nazis. He died either from the torture or by committing suicide, but he never betrayed his comrades.

HENRY J. KAISER (1882 – 1967)

Until World War II, American Henry J. Kaiser had been involved in building bridges, dams, and roads. After the United States entered World War II however, Kaiser used his political influence to win competitive ship-building contracts. Using prefabricated parts and assembly-line techniques in an industry unfamiliar with either, Kaiser's methods focused on speed rather than quality. In this way, Kaiser managed to cut the average time taken to produce a Liberty ship—a basic cargo ship—from 355 days to just 56 days. By the end of the war, Kaiser's shipyards had built more than one-third of all U.S. ships launched during the conflict.

MINNIE VAUTRIN (1886 – 1941)

Born and educated in the United States, Minnie Vautrin sailed to China in 1912 to work as a teacher and Christian missionary. She helped set up and run a school and college for girls at Nanking. When the Japanese Imperial Army invaded Nanking in 1937, Vautrin worked with others to turn the college into a refuge for 10,000 women fleeing Japanese invaders. In spite of heroically saving so many defenseless people, Vautrin was haunted by all those whom she had not managed to help. She wrote, "There is probably no crime that has not been committed in this city." Overwhelmed with horror and disgust at the brutality she had seen, Vautrin committed suicide at home in Illinois.

ANNE FRANK (1929 – 1945)

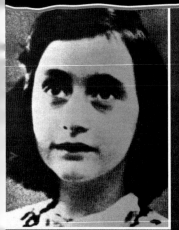

The teenage daughter of a German Jewish family, Anne Frank fled with her parents and sister to Amsterdam in the Netherlands. After the Nazis invaded in 1940, the Franks went into hiding until August 1944. Then they were betrayed, arrested, and sent to a concentration camp along with over 1,000 other Jews from the Netherlands. Anne died from typhus in 1945, at age 15. While Anne was in hiding, she kept a diary describing her fears and her hopes. It was published after the war ended and became internationally famous as a symbol of one girl's enduring faith in herself—and in humanity.

JÓZEF ULM (1900 – 1944)
WIKTORIA ULM (1912 – 1944)

Józef and Wiktoria Ulm were farmers, living in a peaceful village in southeast Poland. When the war started, they agreed to hide eight Jewish civilians from a nearby community, even though sheltering Jews was automatically punished by death in occupied Poland. In 1944, a policeman arranged for the Ulms' house to be searched by German soldiers. First, the Jewish hideaways were discovered and shot, followed by Józef and Wiktoria (who was pregnant). When the six Ulm children saw their parents being killed, they cried in terror. To silence them, the Nazi soldiers brutally killed them all.

CHARITY BICK (1927 – 2002)

Bomb-raid heroine Charity Bick lied about her age and joined the U.K. Air Raid Precautions volunteers when she was only 14. She served as a despatch rider (bicycle messenger). In 1941, she climbed onto a roof to help extinguish a lethal bomb, then cycled four times through gunfire and falling bombs to carry urgent messages. For her courage and determination, Bick was awarded the George Cross, Britain's highest civilian medal. She was the youngest person ever to receive it.

VERA CHALBUR (1914 – 1940)

German spy Vera Chalbur was born to Jewish parents and worked as a night-club dancer in Paris, France. She became friendly with top German secret agents and was recruited as a spy. Her beauty, charm, bravery, and intelligence made her very successful. In 1940, Chalbur was parachuted into Scotland on a secret mission, together with two colleagues. They were all arrested. Chalbur's comrades were executed, but Chalbur disappeared. Historians think that she changed sides and began spying for Britain, helping to defeat the Nazis, but her full story is unknown.

DR. CHARLES DREW (1904 – 1950)

African American doctor and researcher Charles R. Drew was an expert in blood transfusion procedures. He worked to improve techniques used for blood transfusions, safety checking, and storage. He set up the first blood banks to hold large stocks of blood ready to treat injured soldiers and emergency workers. He also campaigned to end racial segregation of blood supplied by donors. In 1940, he played a leading part in the "Blood for Britain" project, set up to treat British casualties at the start of World War II. His work saved countless lives and forever improved how blood products are harvested.

MEMBERS OF THE WOMEN'S VOLUNTEER SERVICE (1938 – 1945)

Founded in 1938 in Britain, the Women's Voluntary Service for Air Raid Precautions was staffed by female volunteers dedicated to helping civilians. In 1939, members helped evacuate more than a million children from big cities. They also ran hostels, clubs, community feeding centers, and first-aid posts. They welcomed and cared for refugees, ran emergency clothing stores, made camouflage nets, handed out ration books, and provided transportation for hospital patients. By 1941, the WVS had a million members. They continued to help those in need during dangerous bombing raids and fires. Many WVS members were awarded medals for bravery; 241 were killed in action.

GLOSSARY

Allied nations The countries that declared war on Nazi Germany in 1939, including Britain, France, and Poland. The Allied nations were aided by their colonies in India, Africa, the Caribbean, Canada, Australia, and New Zealand, and were joined later by the United States and the U.S.S.R.

anschluss The German word for "union." In the buildup to World War II, the term was used to describe the forced union of Germany and Austria.

anti-Semitic Showing hatred of and discrimination against Jews.

appease Used to describe the efforts by British governments in the 1930s to avoid war with Germany.

ARP Air Raid Precautions; the name given to several organized volunteer groups in Britain.

Axis nations The initial alliance of Germany and Italy in 1936, later including Japan and other countries that opposed the Allied powers in World War II.

billeted Sent to live in a particular place on the orders of a government or military authorities.

blackout Measures to stop visible light from houses, shops, factories, and streetlights from escaping into the night sky and guiding enemy bombers to their targets.

blitz The German word for "lightning" that was used during World War II to describe the bombing raids on London.

blitzkrieg The German term used during World War II that means "lightning war."

bloc Group of nations sharing the same political aims or following the same leader. Used to describe the group of nations in Eastern Europe allied with the U.S.S.R. after World War II; Soviet Bloc.

capitalist Supporting political ideas that include freedom for individuals and corporations to own and run businesses, make profits, and create wealth.

cartridge Attachment at the base of a bullet that is packed with the explosives that shoot the bullet.

chancellor Elected leader of a government; Adolf Hitler was the chancellor of Germany from 1933 to 1945.

civilians Men, women, and children who do not belong to any of the armed forces.

communist Follower of writer Karl Marx who believes that the state should own all property and run businesses, industries, schools, hospitals, and other institutions.

concentration camp A prison camp for people whom the authorities wish to remove or separate from society.

doctrine Belief or set of ideas.

Einzatsgruppen Mobile killing squads; Nazi troops sent to execute Jewish communities in north and east Europe.

evacuated Sent away from home to escape the danger of enemy attack.

fire-watchers Civilian volunteers who kept lookout during bombing raids, especially for signs of fire.

gasket Thin layer of compressible material fitted between two parts of a metal joint to seal it and prevent leakage.

ghetto Closed-off neighborhood where living conditions are poor. Usually, ghettoes are home to oppressed or minority communities. In Nazi-occupied Europe during World War II, thousands of Jewish people were forced to live in ghettoes.

Great Depression Worldwide economic crisis that began in 1929 in the United States and lasted for most of the 1930s.

Holocaust Name given by historians to the organized mass slaughter of Jews and other civilian groups by the Nazis.

interned Imprisoned without trial.

mobilized Made ready to fight.

Nazi (National Socialist German Workers') Party Founded in 1919, it was based on militaristic, racial, anti-Semitic and nationalistic policies.

neutral Not taking part in a war.

occupation The invasion and takeover of one country by an enemy nation.

Pearl Harbor A U.S. naval base in Hawaii that the Japanese attacked without warning in December 1941. Much of the U.S. Pacific Fleet was destroyed. The attack led to the United States entry into World War II.

propaganda Media (such as books, newspapers, posters, broadcasts, advertisements, films, and songs) with a persuasive, and often political, message.

radiation sickness Very serious illness caused by radiation from atomic weapons or other radioactive sources. Symptoms include sickness, weakness, extreme fatigue, lowered resistance to infection, and a high risk of developing cancer.

renovation Repairing an object and making it look new.

resigned Accepting a situation without complaint or protest.

socialist Someone who believes that the state should take control of society, run the economy, and limit the powers and profits of rich individuals and businesses.

squalor Conditions including dirt, filth, poverty, and often corruption.

sullen Sulky; angry, silent, and withdrawn.

superpower An extremely powerful state. After World War II, there were only two world superpowers: the United States and the Soviet Union.

tacker Shipyard worker who helped prepare metal parts for welders.

thrifty To save money and avoid waste.

torpedoed Hit (and often sunk) by an underwater bomb, called a torpedo.

U-boats Name, in English, given to German submarines; *U* stands for the German word *untersee*, which means "under sea."

U.S.S.R. The Union of Soviet Socialist Republics; a nation founded after a communist revolution in Russia in 1917. It was made up of many nations, or republics, in Eastern Europe and Central Asia, stretching from the Baltic Sea to the borders of China. The U.S.S.R. supported other communist states all round the world.

welfare A collection of services, such as health care and pensions, run by governments, paid for by taxes, and designed to care for citizens throughout their lives. In Britain, welfare programs were planned by British political leaders during World War II and introduced after the war ended.

Zionists Jewish nationalists whose goal was to build the Jewish state of Israel.

ACKNOWLEDGMENTS

Please visit our web site at: **www.garethstevens.com**.
For a free color catalog describing Gareth Stevens Publishing's
list of high-quality books, call 1-800-542-2595 (USA)
or 1-877-387-3178 (Canada).
Gareth Stevens Publishing's fax: 1-877-542-2596

Library of Congress Cataloging-in-Publication Data

Macdonald, Fiona, 1958-
    World War II: life on the home front: a primary source history /
Fiona Macdonald.
        p. cm. — (In their own words)
    Includes bibliographical references and index.
    ISBN-10: 1-4339-0050-5   ISBN-13: 978-1-4339-0050-1 (lib. bdg.)
    1. United States—History—1933-1945—Juvenile literature.
2. World War, 1939-1945—United States—Juvenile literature.   3.
United States—Social conditions—1933-1945—Juvenile literature.
I. Title.
E806.M216   2008
940.53'73—dc22   2008044084

This North American edition first published in 2009 by
Gareth Stevens Publishing
A Weekly Reader® Company
1 Reader's Digest Road
Pleasantville, NY 10570-7000 USA

Gareth Stevens Executive Managing Editor: Lisa M. Herrington
Gareth Stevens Editor: Joann Jovinelly
Gareth Stevens Creative Director: Lisa Donovan
Gareth Stevens Designers: Giovanni Cipolla, Ken Crossland
Gareth Stevens Production Manager: Paul Bodley, Jr.
Gareth Stevens Publisher: Keith Garton

Photo credits: B=bottom; C=center; L=left; R=right; T=top
20th Century Fox/Everett/Rex Features: 33BR; AElfwine/
Wikimedia Commons: 18B; Age Fotostock/SuperStock: 24T; From
American Goddess at the Rape of Nanking: The Courage of Minnie Vautrin
by Hua-ling Hu (Southern Illinois University Press, 2000): 41B;
Archive of Mateusz Szpytma: 42TR; Miquel Benitez/Rex Features:
17B; Bentley Archives/Popperfoto/Getty Images: 10T; Bettmann/
Corbis: OFCB, 2, 12B, 15T, 24B, 25B, 37B, 38T; Corbis: 30T; CSU
Archives/Everett Collection/Rex Features: 5T; Paul Broadbent/
Alamy: 30B. EPA/Corbis: 40TL; Everett Collection/Rex Features:
43TR; David J. & Janice L. Frent Collection/Corbis: 4BR; Getty
Images: 9B, 10B, 11T, 16, 17T, 20B, 21, 22T, 23, 26B, 27T,
29T, 29B, 31B, 32-33, 33T, 34B, 26B, 39B, 41TL, 43B; Harry S.
Truman Library: 5B; Hulton-Deutsch Collection/Corbis: 13T, 22B,
OFCTR; The Illustrated London News Picture Library, London,
UK/The Bridgeman Art Library: 18T; Imperial War Museum: 28B,
42B; iStock: 6B, 16B, 27B; Mary Evans Picture Library/Alamy:
13B; Minnesota Historical Society/Corbis: OFCTL; The National
Archives: 43TL; National Archives and Records Administration:
19B; Popperfoto/Getty Images: 6T, 10-11, 12T, 34T, 37T; Private
Collection/Look and Learn/The Bridgeman Art Library: 14B, 19T;
Private Collection/Peter Newark Historical Pictures/The Bridgeman
Art Library: 20T; Rex Features: 4BL, 42TL; Shutterstock: 4-5, 6-7,
6B, 39T, 48; SNAP/Rex Features: 32T. Swim Ink 2, LLC/Corbis:
8T, 26T, 31T; Ticktock Media Archive: 4T; Time & Life Pictures/
Getty Images: 7T, 35T, 38BR; Underwood & Underwood/Corbis:
8B; U.S. Navy: 41TR; Wikimedia Commons: 40R.

Every effort has been made to trace the copyright holders. We
apologize in advance for any unintentional ommissions. We would be
pleased to insert the appropriate acknowledgments in any subsequent
edition of this publication.

Printed in the United States of America

1 2 3 4 5 6 7 8 9 10 10 09 08